ABUNDANT BLESSINGS FROM A BROKEN SOUL

MARISSA PENNINGTON

urbanpress

Abundant Blessings From A Broken Soul
by Marissa Pennington
Copyright ©2022 Marissa Pennington

ISBN 978-1-63360-197-0

Scripture quotations are taken from THE HOLY BIBLE: New International Version ©1978 by the New York International Bible Society, used by permission of Zondervan Bible Publishers. All rights reserved.

For Worldwide Distribution
Printed in the U.S.A.

Urban Press
P.O. Box 8881
Pittsburgh, PA 15221-0881
412.646.2780

DEDICATIONS

Dedicated to my daughter, my legacy, Eliana Li.
—Marissa Pennington

Dedicated to my daughter, Savannah Grace.
You make me brave; I love you.
—Rebecca Danielle

CONTENTS

FOREWORD

The National Association of Adult Survivors of Child Abuse (NAASCA) estimates 42 million adults are survivors of childhood sexual abuse and of those, 20% were abused under the age of eight. It is further estimated that 90% were abused by someone they knew, loved, and trusted.* The CDC believes that 50% of children will experience some type of abuse; sexual, physical, emotional, or neglect. Most survivors suffer alone in silence, never telling anyone of the horrific and terrifying experiences they lived through. If they did tell an adult of the abuse, they were often not believed, blamed for the abuse, or ignored. The effects of prolonged and untreated childhood abuse are multifaceted, causing a multitude of emotional, relational, spiritual, physical, and mental health problems.

I am a Licensed Mental Health Counselor and Licensed Chemical Dependency Professional and Certified Professional Christian Counselor. I have been counseling for more than 40 years, treating adults with substance abuse disorders, codependence, anxiety, suicidal ideation, self-harming behaviors, depression, personality disorders, and relationship issues. The majority of my clients coming for treatment have histories of child abuse. Very often I am the first person they share their painful stories with.

It takes great courage to share traumatic experiences. They can easily become flooded with emotions as they begin to unload the horrors of their childhood. Shame, fear, anger, and grief are the common feelings resulting from their childhood trauma. But there is hope. It is through sharing that

---

*www.naasca.org

healing can begin. I know this not only through my experience as a therapist but also as a survivor myself.

There was a time in my youth that I wanted to die. The abuse I suffered at the hand of my father and others left me feeling worthless, shamed, and overwhelmed with fear. I felt hopeless and I prayed that God would take my life—and He did when I was born again! And what man intended for evil God used for His glory as I spent my entire career helping others find healing too.

There is a saying in the twelve-step community that "you're only as sick as your secrets." You are not alone. The author of this book, Marissa Pennington, is a dear friend. She discovered through much prayer and counseling the healing power of telling her story and journaling. Now through the leading of the Holy Spirit, she shares the depth of her pain and the journey of healing in this book of poems. My prayer for you is that as you read Marissa's book, you will know you are not alone. There is hope for you to experience a life with purpose and joy.

Linda J. Gil CAADC, LCDP, LMHC
Warwick, Rhode Island

ABUNDANT BLESSINGS FROM A BROKEN SOUL

A WORD FROM THE AUTHOR

I have suffered from depression and anxiety my entire life. They have always been a battle for me, which is the reason this book of poems is so important to me. You see, I wrote them all in a time of desperation. In January 2021, I found out I was pregnant with our second child and I was so excited, but unfortunately the pregnancy was not viable. I went into a state of utter depression, anxiety, self-harm, and suicidal ideations. I was diagnosed with Major Depressive Disorder, PTSD, anxiety with agoraphobia, and a form of borderline personality disorder.

My therapist and NP decided to put me into a day program at the hospital. At first, I was completely against it because, quite frankly, I was terrified I would be committed. I was convinced they would lock the door and throw away the key. Eventually, however, God brought me to a place of acceptance—accepting it for what it was. I slowly realized that this was meant to help and not hurt me.

A few days before I was to start the program, I wrote a letter to God describing how angry I was at Him—angry for everything I had gone through in my life and how much I had suffered because of it. At the end of my letter, while crying my eyes out, God put a poem on my heart. I realized what the writers of the psalms must have experienced, for many of them were crying out to God and what happened?

They ended up writing things that people still read and draw strength from today.

Now to me, this was definitely a God-thing because I had never written a single poem in my life and I certainly wasn't expecting to do so at that moment when I was pouring my heart out to Him. Actually, I don't even like to write and here I am with a book of poems. Only God . . .

Every poem in this book tells my story of all I have gone through in life, things I have felt and things I have done. After each poem is a short synopsis of why I wrote the poem and also a short journal entry area to challenge you to write about your own experiences—and maybe even a poem of your own. Whatever you are going through, I urge you to do what I did—go to God and tell Him exactly how you feel. He already knows, so it's not for His benefit, it's for yours.

These poems are so very personal to me and I consider them to be inspired by God. I consider each one His gift to me and now to you. I pray this book blesses you as it has blessed me.

Marissa Pennington
Coventry, Rhode Island
July 2022

A WORD FROM
THE PHOTOGRAPHER

Photography has always been so much more than an art form to me. It is a way to still the precious moments that arc fleeting and ever-changing, and a chance to revisit these moments again. Most often we want to capture the light and the beauty in life, things like our newborn babies or school graduations. Through pictures, we can stop and gaze at the happy memories as reminders of the goodness in our lives. Sometimes photos remind us of difficult seasons as well. Looking back at the dark times reminds us that we overcame those challenges and that our lives are not static or still. We get another shot each day to create a good picture.

I've always had a passion for photography but I was inspired to make it my career after my daughter was born. We've had quite the journey, just the two of us, and though there have been many struggles, it has also been filled with so much joy. I was always behind the camera trying to capture my daughter's beauty but I wanted moments with just the two of us as well. When I started hiring photographers to take our pictures, I was so grateful that even a small amount of our loving bond could be seen and shared! The pictures were so priceless to me that I decided I wanted to duplicate this feeling for others by helping them capture their special moments.

My secret to get through life has always been to find the light and focus on the beauty, so photography comes naturally to me. Marissa's poetry was the inspiration for the photography in this book. The poems reminded me that the darkness in life may overwhelm us at times, but the light will prevail. I give God all the credit for my successes, for He's never left my side during the black, white, and even gray moments of my life.

Rebecca Danielle
Cranston, Rhode Island

BOTTOMLESS

Anger, hurt, pain
and why must there be so much shame?

It's all stuffed way down inside,
and all I want to do is hide.

It's like a well with no bottom
where I've deposited all my deep, deep sorrow.

I need to scream or cry or shout,
but even then, I'm not sure I'll get it all out.

God, I'm turning back to You in need
since everything else has just caused me to bleed.

I want to call You Father again
as I did way back when it all began.

I must believe,
I must know
that anything to You
is possible to show.

"I consider that our present sufferings are not worth comparing with the glory that will be revealed in us" – Romans 8:18.

Have you ever felt like you had so much pain inside you that it would never end? That there was no bottom to your sadness? That is how I felt for more than 35 years. I had so much pain stuffed deep down inside me that it was nearly impossible to get it out of me and into the open. However, with the help of God and a few very close friends I trusted, I was able to dig out of the empty hole I had fallen into.

JOURNAL ENTRY

Have you ever felt like your situation or pain had no bottom? If so, write about that time. Be specific about how you felt and how you felt about God while you were going through it.

_____

_____

_____

_____

_____

_____

_____

A DISTANT SOUL

I was distant throughout my life,
distant throughout my strife.

It began when I was six,
when other things got in the mix.

I was distant through all the gifts;
I was distant through all the conflicts.

How can I be a distant soul?
That contradicts
God's desire to console,
for He is whole
and I have a hole
that only He can fill in His role.

A distant soul I was,
a distant soul I am
'cause of all the cuts and scars
that I hid under His stars.

A distant soul I will no longer be—
a distant soul I can no longer be.

As my Father fills my heart,
I will no longer be apart—
as my Father fills my heart.

*"By day the Lord directs his love, at night his song is with me—
a prayer to the God of my life" – Psalm 42:8.*

Someone once told me I have always been distant, never opening up about my feelings or anything I was going through. It's true but I had a reason to be distant. There was trauma in my life that started when I was six and it shaped my entire being from that point on. It made me scared to say anything, made me feel like no one would believe me. It is amazing how a traumatic event you remember from such a young age can cause so much hurt and pain so many years later. It took more than 30 years for me to even tell one person what had happened to me. That all led to a long road of depression, anxiety, and PTSD that I finally had to face. The process has not been easy and has even created a few more scars, but God was and is with me through it all. When we take steps forward, He is with us. When we take steps backwards, He is with us. God is always good.

JOURNAL ENTRY

Write about a time you felt God was not with you but in the end you realized He really was.

_____

_____

_____

_____

_____

DADDY'S-LITTLE-GIRL

Was I ever your little girl,
as precious as a pearl?

I didn't feel it;
I didn't know it.
I only wished you had shown it.

When I needed your protection,
where were you?
When I needed your assurance,
where were you?
When I needed your love,
where were you?

I turned to other things
and other flings.
But the emptiness still brings
hurt, sadness, anger, and pain—
which I let out in acts of vain.

Daddy's-little-girl!
I never was and never will be,
but I have a new Daddy
who allows me to be me.

He loves me through it all
even when I fall.
He loves me through it all
even when I stall.
He loves me through it all
even when I don't answer His call.

I am His daddy's-little-girl
through it all,
through it all.
I am His Daddy's-little-girl.

ABUNDANT BLESSINGS FROM A BROKEN SOUL

"'I will be a Father to you, and you will be my sons and daughters,' says the Lord Almighty" – 2 Corinthians 6:18.

Were you daddy's little girl? I wish I was. I always longed to be my daddy's little girl but we never had a close relationship. I had everything I could ever need or want materialistically, but not emotionally. I never had a hug, a kiss on the cheek, or an "I love you" from my earthly father and that affected me throughout my entire life. I had to find God, and when I did, I finally felt like I was daddy's little girl—like I was truly loved and cared for by God our Father in heaven.

JOURNAL ENTRY

Your heavenly Father loves and cares for you, too. Write a letter to your Father in heaven and tell Him how you feel about Him.

_____

_____

_____

_____

_____

_____

_____

ABUNDANT BLESSINGS FROM A BROKEN SOUL

ABUNDANT BLESSINGS FROM A BROKEN SOUL

HIDDEN

Dealing with pain
is not something you want to gain.
But unfortunately it's a part of life,
having to deal with so much strife.

Some people go through a lot,
while others don't know what they got.
When the pain is so unbearable,
what can I do to not make it wearable?

It doesn't show on the outside,
but if you could only see me on the inside—
the hurt, the anguish, the sadness,
the pressure to keep quiet the madness.

What do I do?
Where do I go?

I knew in my mind
who I needed to find,
but my mind was not right
perhaps out of spite.

The hatred, the anger, I poured upon myself,
putting God on the shelf.

Sharp edges on my skin
instead was the sin.
Sliding across my arm
releasing, releasing, releasing,
I thought was the charm
but it only brought more harm.

Until one day,
I wrote God a letter
with the hope of it making me feel better.

I said to Him,
"I'm angry
I'm hurt
I'm sad
I'm abandoned."

Why God did you abandon me?
And He said in return,
"You abandoned me."

The light went on and I felt the pressure release;
now finally I feel at peace.

They keep saying to me, "Where is the word of the Lord?
Let it now be fulfilled!" – Jeremiah 17:15.

I hid my trauma from when I was a kid until age 35. All those years of hiding really damaged me on the inside. All the sadness and anger were stuffed so deep down inside that they created a pressure I could not figure out how to release. When I started talking about the trauma in my adult years, the pressure had become unbearable. Instead of learning how to release it in a healthy way, I ended up releasing it in an unhealthy way through cutting my arms with scissors. It gave me relief from the pressure for a short time, but what followed that action were shame and guilt. After I wrote my letter to God, I realized I was the one who abandoned Him; He had never left my side. Since that incident, I still struggle but I have learned to release it in these poems and writings.

JOURNAL ENTRY

What are some healthy/unhealthy ways you release pain? If unhealthy, try to list some alternative healthy ways to release it.

_____

_____

_____

_____

_____

ABUNDANT BLESSINGS FROM A BROKEN SOUL

THE MOURNING

There's a part inside me that I dislike;
"You don't want to know what she's like."

She hates, she harms,
she downright alarms.
When she's in control,
I have no self-control.

She must go, she must flee
but part of me hears her plea:
"Hold on to me, hold on tight.
Don't let go; it will be a fight."

A fight it has been to the core;
a fight it is, an ongoing war.

But one day God said, "I will restore
as I have so much more in store."

I'm glad
but I'm sad,
and part of me is mad.

I want her to stay;
I don't want her to go.
But God said you must,
or it will be a blow.

Slowly but surely I'm letting her leave.
Slowly but surely I know I can't cleave.

I'm mourning my need to destroy
but I know now I will enjoy
the joy that comes in the morning.

"Sing the praises of the Lord, you his faithful people; praise his holy name. For his anger lasts only a moment, but his favor lasts a lifetime; weeping may stay for the night, but rejoicing comes in the morning" – Psalm 30:4-5.

As I was writing these poems, I felt like a part of me was dying and I was mourning the loss. I wasn't happy, I wasn't excited, I was actually sad. The part of me that hated me, that wanted to destroy me, was slowly being transformed and that was hard for me because she was with me my entire life. She was all I really knew. The other part of me that wanted to be happy and joyful was new to me. I really didn't know who she was or how to be. But to me this was life or death. Through this journey, I'm finding out who I am and who God created me to be.

JOURNAL ENTRY

Write about something the loss of which you may be mourning, even though you want to leave it—or maybe even want to hang on to—but it must go.

_____

_____

_____

_____

_____

_____

ABUNDANT BLESSINGS FROM A BROKEN SOUL

FLY LITTLE BIRDS

Fly little birds,
fly high in the sky.

Up to the heavens above,
where you are made as white as a dove.

God called you home,
long before I could have known.

Fly little birds,
fly high in the sky.

I long for the day
when my tears fade away.

I will see you again,
but I don't know when

I never met you,
I never held you,
I never hugged or kissed you.
But I knew this from the start
that you will always be in my heart.

Fly little birds,
fly high in the sky.

*"Forget the former things; do not dwell on the past.
See, I am doing a new thing! Now it springs up; do you not
perceive it? I am making a way in the wilderness and streams
in the wasteland" — Isaiah 43:18-19.*

I have two little birds flying high in heaven because I miscarried two babies. The first one was via IVF and the baby's heart stopped beating when I was nine weeks pregnant. Then my little rainbow baby, Eliana, came via IVF and she has been my biggest blessing. Then in early 2021, I became pregnant naturally and it was a big surprise! We were quite excited and happy, but unfortunately it turned out that the pregnancy wasn't viable. The fetus had a very slow heart rate and it stopped beating the day after we saw it on the monitor. I was devastated, sad, and mad, and couldn't understand why God would do that to me. Why would He punish me? I know it's just a part of life but it was extremely painful—and at times still is. I never let this second baby go, so this poem is for both my babies as I let them fly high and free into the heavens.

JOURNAL ENTRY

Is there something or someone you need to let go of?
If so, write about it.

_____

_____

_____

_____

ABUNDANT BLESSINGS FROM A BROKEN SOUL

A TINY MIRACLE

A tiny miracle
who she longed to come.

Years of praying,
years of waiting,
but the years started fading.

The years became too many to count,
and for not much did they amount.

Until one day
in a hospital bay,
a glimmer of hope,
a glimmer of light
was such a delightful sight.

After much trial and error,
medicine and injections to prepare her.

Physical, mental, and emotional pain
but it was never done in vain.

It was to have you by her side,
a tiny miracle that God did provide.

Perfect in every way—
Tiny hands, tiny eyes, tiny nose, tiny mouth, tiny feet—
God created you so very complete.

"Take delight in the Lord, and he will give you the desires of your heart" – Psalm 37:4.

My tiny miracle is named Eliana Li, which in Hebrew means "God answered to me." God answered my many, many prayers for a little one of my own to care for and love. She was conceived via IVF which is a very painful physical and emotional process with much medication and many injections to prepare my body for a baby. After about three rounds of IVF, we finally received our miracle baby who is perfect and healthy in every way.

JOURNAL ENTRY

Write about a miracle/prayer God has answered for you or that you are still waiting for Him to answer.

_____

_____

_____

_____

_____

_____

_____

ABUNDANT BLESSINGS FROM A BROKEN SOUL

THROUGH THE PROCESS

A sadness so deep,
I can hardly weep.

A sadness so hopeless,
it makes me feel so soul-less.

Why, oh, why
can I not cry?

Is it even real?
Why can't I feel?

It's buried so deep inside me
that there's nowhere to run or hide from me.

It wants to come out, it wants to explode,
before I decide to lay down and implode.

God help me release;
this sadness must cease

I must decrease,
He must increase
in order to have this sadness deceased.

I trust in Your process,
though I see little progress.

But I know you are working
even though I'm hurting.

I trust You with all my heart
because I never want to be apart—
from Your love,
Your grace—
I'm determined to win this race.

Being confident of this, that he who began a good work in you will carry it on to completion until the day of Christ Jesus
– Philippians 1:6.

Have you ever felt so sad that you couldn't even cry? The grief was pushed down so deep inside that if you cried or let it out, you had no idea what would happen? This is exactly how I felt in the midst of the lowest points of my depression. There were many times I wanted to explode, to just yell and scream, but I couldn't. I was afraid—afraid of what would happen. How would I react? Would I act on urges that I already struggled with? But God . . . He helped me find a release in a healthy way. I knew I had to decrease and let His spirit increase in me. I had to let Him take over and *trust Him*! Even when we do not see or feel Him working, *He is.*

JOURNAL ENTRY

Write about something you could not or cannot cry about, and release it to God as you write.

_____

_____

_____

_____

_____

_____

ABUNDANT BLESSINGS FROM A BROKEN SOUL

QUESTIONING REALITY

A sadness so deep:
What's real?
What's not?
Why must some stir the pot?

My reality may not be yours,
yours may not be mine.

You wonder:
How can that be?
Why didn't I see?
Anything you say mustn't be.

So I question my reality:
Did I make it all up
just to pump it up?

But God said, "No,
it's not just a show.
It's the real deal
that I am going to heal.

"I'm revealing things you never knew
because I have a plan for you.

"To help others in the same boat
'cause of what you wrote.

"I love you, my daughter,
I'm making you stronger.

"I am growing you up
and filling your cup."

"Peace I leave with you; my peace I give you. I do not give to you as the world gives. Do not let your hearts be troubled and do not be afraid" – John 14:27.

I was carrying a trauma that was hidden for 35 years of my life. When I finally came clean, someone close said to me, "How can that be?" and "I don't see how that could have happened." Their doubt made me question reality. Did I make it up? God reassured me, however, that I didn't make it up. I experienced traumatic things in my life. I know now why: to grow up with a damaged little girl inside me, to write this book, to encourage other women, to help other women get through similar situations.

JOURNAL ENTRY

Did you ever tell someone you trusted something but they didn't believe you, which hurt you deeply? It made you question whether you really experienced it or not? Write about what you went through.

_____

_____

_____

_____

_____

_____

ABUNDANT BLESSINGS FROM A BROKEN SOUL

A CRITICAL MOMENT

There was a critical moment in time
when I had to make a choice.
I don't know how I made the climb
but I know it gave me a voice.

I had to choose to live not die—
to revive, not deprive—
to fly high and not let it pass me by.

Nothing in this world comes easy.
The work has to be done even if it
makes me queasy.

The urges to cut
only kept the door shut.

Dealing with the pain,
I had to try to stay sane.

I kept God as my source
so I could stay the course.

I stayed in His Word,
completely submerged.

When that occurred,
I know I heard
God say,
"In this critical moment, I emerged
and gave you the strength to be undeterred."

"For whoever wants to save their life will lose it, but whoever loses their life for me will find it" – Matthew 16:25.

While in a recovery program, I needed to make a choice: to live or to die. It felt as if it was that stark and urgent. I chose life, but I had to do the work—the work the program asked of me, the work mentally and emotionally, and the work spiritually. It hasn't been easy but it's been worth it. Through it all, I stay in God's Word, no matter the strife. He has been with me even more so in every critical moment.

JOURNAL ENTRY

Did you ever have the feeling that you needed to make a choice, to choose between life and death? What did you choose to do metaphorically—or even literally?

_____

_____

_____

_____

_____

_____

_____

WORK IT OUT

When in doubt,
I will work it out.

Don't get caught up in the sadness,
I will turn it into gladness.

Quiet the anger
for I am your anchor.

When in despair
know I will repair.

In the moments of crying
I'm at work supplying.

With temptations of harm,
remember I'm your charm.

In the midst of alarms,
I come with open arms.

When you desire to be in the arms of death,
just know I'm as close as your breath.

I love you, My child.
Even all the while,
I feel your pain, I feel your doubt.
But know, I will always help you work it out.

In him we were also chosen, having been predestined according to the plan of him who works out everything in conformity with the purpose of his will, in order that we, who were the first to put our hope in Christ, might be for the praise of his glory
— Ephesians 1:11-12.

I was terrified to begin a day program at the hospital, but as I started, God worked out my fears and my temptation to run. He started quieting my mind and I accepted where I was and what I had to do to get healed. I needed to put in the work, and then He would work—and that is exactly what happened. I submitted to the program and the doctors, was completely honest about everything, and God worked it all out!

JOURNAL ENTRY

Can you recall an instance that you were resisting and finally submitted to the process, and God worked it out in your best interest?

_____

_____

_____

_____

_____

THE CLIMB

Now is the time
to start the climb.

Out of the valley,
out of the alley,
up the mountain, to the top—
where I'm praying my head will stop.

The voices, the noises, the shadows, the screams!
I hope it will then feel like only bad dreams.

It's time for a change;
this can't stay the same.

Your healing I want.
Your healing I'll take.
Your healing is free for all of our sake.

So now is the time
to start the climb.

You opened the door,
I can see what's in store.

I'll praise You through this
no matter how hard.
I'll praise You through this
no matter how scarred.

So now is the time
to start the climb.

"He lifted me out of the slimy pit, out of the mud and mire; he set my feet on a rock and gave me a firm place to stand"
— Psalm 40:2.

It was time. I was ready to climb out of my pit! It took a while, a long while, but it was time for my healing. It was work and a lot of it. It was exhausting mentally and physically, but God was with me all along the way. He opened a door for me to accept healing and I took it. I do not know how many doors God opened that I never walked through, but I walked through this one and I wasn't turning back.

JOURNAL ENTRY

Write about a situation out of which God helped you escape and thank Him for the open door.

ABUNDANT BLESSINGS FROM A BROKEN SOUL

HOLDING YOUR HAND

I'm holding Your hand
so I can stand.
I'm holding on tight
with all of my might.

Hold me through these times of trouble,
then I know my blessings will double.

There are so many things to unroll,
so many things to unfold,
so many things the enemy stole.
But I believe in what You foretold
that there are many things yet to behold.

If I try to release
and I try to cease,
take my hand
so I can feel Your peace.

You're holding my hand
so I can stand.
I'm holding on tight
with all of my might.

You won't let me stumble,
you won't let me fall.
Even if I have to crawl,
I promise I won't stall.

I might fight
out of spite,
but shine Your light
through my darkest night.

Your hand will never let me go
even when the tears flow.

Thank You, Lord, for Your grace,
I surely feel Your embrace
as I seek Your face.

For I am the Lord your God who takes hold of your right hand and says to you, Do not fear; I will help you. – Isaiah 41:13.

I wrote this poem after I received a text from a friend in which she said God was holding onto my wrists and not letting go! I surely let go plenty of times but this time God had me in a way where I couldn't break free, even if I tried. You cannot let go of someone who is holding your wrists. So He was with me through all the stumbles, falls, crawls, and stalls. He was there with me the whole time, holding onto me and determined never to let me go.

JOURNAL ENTRY

Do you believe God was/is holding on to you with all His might through something you were/are going through?
Write about it.

_____

_____

_____

_____

_____

_____

_____

ACCEPTANCE

Must I accept who I am?
Or do I need to do what I can
to push through, to feel whole,
even though it feels out of control?

The depression
turns into obsession.
The anxiety
takes the breath right out of me.

Do I accept or do I resist?
Not sure which way to exist.
To live or to die,
both make me want to run and hide.

I must accept the things I can't change,
the pain and sadness I can't seem to exchange.
I must accept
all the times I have wept
while God has kept me
and has never slept.

God is my light in the dark.
He is that little spark
that wants to leave a mark
and be my one and only rock.

Accept one another, then, just as Christ accepted you, in order to bring praise to God – Romans 15:7.

It's funny that I wrote the title of this poem days before I had any inspiration to write anything else. I ended up writing this after one of my day session programs where we talked about acceptance. It's interesting how God works and puts a thought on my heart and then brings it into fulfillment a few days later.

JOURNAL ENTRY

Write down something that might be a thought in your mind right now and then come back a few days later and see if you can expand on it.

_____

_____

_____

_____

_____

_____

_____

_____

BARRIERS

Why are barriers her norm
all throughout the storm?
So annoyed
because she feels null and void.

No emotion
is ever put in motion
because of fear,
because of strife—
she feels she has no life.

The barriers are what carry her;
one day the barriers might bury her.

They put up a wall
and all she can do is crawl
to do what she needs to do—
it's a battle just to get through,

She fights with all her might
just to stay out of sight.
To feel safe, to feel secure,
there is only One who can ensure.

God is her light, God is her strength;
to show His love He goes to great length.

With Him the barriers break;
with Him the barriers shake.
With Him the barriers come crashing down;
with Him she won't be backing down.

For he himself is our peace, who has made the two groups one and has destroyed the barrier, the dividing wall of hostility
– Ephesians 2:14.

I had barriers that either stopped me or tried stopping me from doing things. The biggest was fear of people and feeling in danger due to my childhood trauma. I hated calling people on the phone, I would rather text. I could not get out of my car at the store when I was alone until there were no people around. I wouldn't walk down an aisle in a store if people were there, but I had to force myself to do these things in order to get my errands done. Only God and my faith and trust in Him broke down those barriers!

JOURNAL ENTRY

What barriers do you have and how do you think you can break them down?

_____

_____

_____

_____

_____

_____

Abundant Blessings From A Broken Soul

FASCINATION

A fascination with death,
a fascination with a last breath.

Why God why
are these feelings inside?
At times I want to cry;
at times I want to die.
At other times I want to try
to stay alive and thrive.

An obsession with the death thought
is something I've always fought.

What does it feel like?
Is there regret?
Is there pain?
Is there any shame?

As I sit here and write this
there's a feeling I cannot miss.
I don't want to know how it feels,
I don't want to have a regret,
I don't want to feel the pain
for all would have been done in vain.

I can no longer be fascinated with death;
I want to be fascinated with Your Spirit's breath.

I want to live,
I want to survive.
God, please revive
for I know You never deprive.

Fill me again with your Spirit;
fill me again with your joy,
the joy I long to employ.

A fascination with life
is now what I possess.
I lived, I survived,
but I have not yet arrived.

God, You are good
even after all I've withstood.
God, You are good;
all the time, God, You are good.

What agreement is there between the temple of God and idols? For we are the temple of the living God. As God has said: "I will live with them and walk among them and I will be their God, and they will be my people" – 2 Corinthians 6:16.

At first I thought, "Maybe this poem is too morbid to put into this book?" But I realized it wasn't, it was truth and it ends with choosing life over death. It has been something I have struggled with for so long—the thoughts and fascination of death—and I never knew why. I still don't know why. But now, I'm choosing to be fascinated with life and no longer the former.

JOURNAL ENTRY

Do you have a fascination with something that affects you in an unhealthy way? If so, write about it and pray for God to remove that thing from your life.

_____

_____

_____

_____

_____

_____

_____

ABUNDANT BLESSINGS FROM A BROKEN SOUL

IN THE MOMENT

Why does the thought of being mindful
sound so terribly frightful?
Is it because it's about being in the moment
when all I want to do is disown it?

My mind wanders left and right;
it can't see what's in my line of sight.

Why is it so hard
when my thoughts bombard
and just leave me scarred?

It's about being purposeful,
which sounds so learnable.
But numbness prevails
and when I'm on autopilot,
nothing else can avail.

And I still go to and fro,
any which way my mind wants to go.
God, help me to be intentional
which sounds so unconventional.

The thought of being mindful
won't be so frightful;
it will become delightful.

I thank You, Lord,
for all You've restored,
for all that You poured.
Your love has me floored.

For we live by faith, not by sight — 2 Corinthians 5:7.

I never thought about mindfulness until I entered my program. It means to purposely be in the moment of whatever it is I am doing, even if it is something simple like doing laundry or washing dishes. My mind was always all over the place, thinking about what was coming or what I had to do next. It was always going, going, going. I realized that was because I was avoiding other thoughts that may pop in my head, thoughts of things I didn't want to think about. I always kept my mind going to protect myself and keep other thoughts out. Sometimes distractions can be good, but when they become disassociation and happen all the time (which was how it was with me), then it becomes very unhealthy. Learning this was like a lightbulb going on above my head.

JOURNAL ENTRY

Are you mindful or do you distract yourself constantly to the point of disassociation? Write about what that feels like and what you think it has cost you.

_____

_____

_____

_____

_____

_____

OBSERVER SELF

How do you see yourself?
Are you all in good health?
Or do you put yourself on a shelf?

I observed myself from the outside
and what I saw on the inside
was hate, guilt, and shame—
from which I felt blame.

I had to do something,
I couldn't do nothing.
I had to reconnect
to my Father whom I did neglect.

I turned back to Him
and it wasn't on a whim.
I wanted to be mindful,
I wanted to watch
Him make me top notch.

I prayed,
I stayed,
I obeyed.

Then He said to me;
"You are beautiful in My eyes
do not believe all the lies.
You are not to blame
or the cause of your pain."

"I am here to take it away
and not just for today.
Keep your eyes on Me
and you will always be free—
that I can guarantee."

"For you created my inmost being; you knit me together in my mother's womb. I praise you because I am fearfully and wonderfully made; your works are wonderful, I know that full well"
— Psalm 139:13-14.

How do you see yourself? For me, I hated myself. Others saw me from the outside, the smile, the laugh, looking like I had no worries at all. But that was all a facade. Inside, I was full of hate, guilt, and shame about myself. I pushed God aside and isolated myself from others until I realized I could no longer keep living that way. I needed to be real, to show others what I am going through on the inside, not just to help myself, but to help and encourage others. I gave this testimony in a Thanksgiving church service where I was real and raw, and I found that freeing for me. It was not easy, but afterwards, I received a lot of feedback about how brave it was and how it encouraged others, which was my prayer. Know that God sees you as His precious daughter or son even when you don't see it. You are His greatest joy.

JOURNAL ENTRY

How do you see yourself? Is it positive or negative? Would God agree with how you feel about yourself? What do you need to change? Write about it.

_____

_____

_____

_____

ABUNDANT BLESSINGS FROM A BROKEN SOUL

WORTH FAR MORE

Having compassion for others
is an easy thing to do.
Having compassion for myself,
well, I always put that on the shelf.

It's compassion versus judgment,
the latter is an indulgement.

It's connection versus isolation,
I preferred the separation.

It's self-kindness versus hostility
the latter was my probability.

It's hard to imagine
validation comes with compassion
which is what I needed to re-examine.

To be understood,
to be reassured
my safety secured,
and to know that all is good.
I cannot rely on others
in order to be recovered.

God is my companion,
God is my validation,
God is my connection,
to lead me in the right direction.

He said; "Be kind to yourself.
Don't get caught up with everything else.

"My daughter, in My eyes you shine.
Can't you see the signs?

"Compassion versus judgment
Now the former will be your indulgement.

"Connection versus isolation
you need the integration
with my loving ways and affection.

"Self-kindness versus hostility
The first will now be your ability.
You are worth far more
and now it's time to soar."

For God so loved the world that he gave his one and only Son, that whoever believes in him shall not perish but have eternal life
– John 3:16.

Compassion has always been a hard thing for me to extend to myself. I could easily be compassionate towards others, but to myself—never! The opposite of compassion is judgment and I would always prefer to judge myself than to be kind to myself. But we are God's creation! More specifically, I am God's creation. He not only wants us to care for our physical bodies but also our minds and emotions! In this poem I started with the negative being the way I thought but in the end, with the help of God, the negative became positive.

JOURNAL ENTRY

Are you kind to yourself on a daily basis? If so, explain how. If not, write how you can be more compassionate to yourself.

_____

_____

_____

_____

_____

_____

_____

AFTER THE STORM

After the storm,
where do I go?
What do I do?
Am I now transformed?

A month in this place,
I had to seek Your face.
No matter how hard,
no matter how scarred,
I laid it all down
in front of You, God.

I wept and wept
but You I always kept
in my heart,
in my sight—
even in my fight.

You calmed my storm and
even the waves conformed.
I thank You, Lord,
for all that You poured,
all that You restored.
And now You I adore.

Now I reflect
about all I had to accept.
After the storm,
I know where to go,
I know what to do.
Because you love me,
now I can see,
for You made me
perfect and free.

"I have revealed and saved and proclaimed—I, and not some foreign god among you. You are my witnesses," declares the Lord, "that I am God" – Isaiah 43:12.

It was bittersweet for me when I left the program. I felt safe there. I felt I had a voice and was understood. As my time there came to an end, I was unsure of what was to come next. I was afraid of backsliding and going back to the same place I was in when I began the program. After this storm, where do I go? I had to keep my eyes on Jesus, like Peter did when he walked on water, and not look away. Otherwise, I would surely fall. My eyes are now open to all God has in store for me going forward.

JOURNAL ENTRY

Write about a time you took your eyes off Jesus and fell. When you fixed your eyes back on Him, what happened?

_____

_____

_____

_____

_____

_____

ABUNDANT BLESSINGS FROM A BROKEN SOUL

TIME TO BREATHE

Now is the time to let out a breath,
to rest, and no longer be stressed.

With all of my strength,
with all of God's grace,
I worked at length
and at a steady pace.

Now is the time to let out a breath,
as You have given me the time to invest.
I was pushed, I was pressed,
no longer depressed.

I progressed,
I passed the test—
I feel so blessed!
Thank You, Lord,
for giving me rest.

"Be still, and know that I am God; I will be exalted among the nations, I will be exalted in the earth" – Psalm 46:10.

When I wrote this poem, this was *not* at all how I felt! I was writing this about my future self. I was thinking about how I was letting God work in me and was praying this is how I would be after I finished the day program. Thank God for grace. It was no easy task, but God is always good. He sees us through the hardest times and gives us moments to breathe before, during, and after.

JOURNAL ENTRY

When was a point in your life you were able to take a breath and be at peace with whatever you were going through?

_____

_____

_____

_____

_____

_____

_____

FREE

I am free
I am free
Finally I am free

I soar like an eagle in the sky
With my wings held high

I am free
I am free
Finally I am free

I am like a dove
My heart full of love

I am free
I am free
Finally I am free

I shine bright and still
Like a city on a hill

I am free
I am free
Finally I am free

At peace with myself
No longer fighting my past or my other self.

I am free
I am free
Finally I am free

You are my world
As precious as a pearl

You are my all in all
I have answered Your call

You are my all in all
Not putting up any more walls

You are my all in all
I will always recall

I am free
I am free
Finally I am free

Now the Lord is the Spirit, and where the Spirit of the Lord is, there is freedom — 2 Corinthians 3:17.

What does it mean to be free? No more pain? No more depression? Then unfortunately, we will always have struggles in life. But to be free in Jesus means we can make it through all our tough times as long as we lean on Him. He will be there to listen, to lift us up, to walk with us. He is the one constant that must be in our lives. He gives us the freedom to run, dance, and be joyful in all things. I am free! I am finally free!

JOURNAL ENTRY

Do you feel as if you are free in Jesus? Do you have a relationship with Him? If so, write about how you were saved. If not, write a prayer asking God into your heart.

_____

_____

_____

_____

_____

_____

_____

Abundant Blessings From A Broken Soul

BLESSED BEYOND MEASURE

Am I blessed beyond measure
knowing all my treasure?

Am I blessed beyond measure
with things that give me pleasure?

Yes, I am blessed;
I should not be stressed.

God always provides,
He also presides,
and wants to reside
in my heart
as a work of art.

"Trust Me and see;
I guarantee

"I Am caring for you.
I Am there for you.
I Am good for you."

Am I blessed beyond measure
knowing all of my treasure?

Am I blessed beyond measure
with things that give me pleasure?

Yes, I am blessed;
He always gives me His best.

Every good and perfect gift is from above, coming down from the Father of the heavenly lights, who does not change like shifting shadows – James 1:17.

Am I blessed even through all my strife? Yes I am and so are you! God provides and cares for us. He is not a respecter of persons. His blessings are meant for all and they are always His best. We tend to forget that and sometimes not believe it, especially in times of strife. But *believe* and *know* that God is good all the time and all the time, God is good.

JOURNAL ENTRY

Write about all the ways God has blessed you.

_____

_____

_____

_____

_____

_____

_____

_____

_____

THE TRANSFORMATION

Who will I be
after You change me?

Will I still be me?
Will I feel free?

In this moment,
I don't know me.
In this moment,
my plea
is that You make me like You,
make me anew.

Who will I be
after You change me?

The sun will shine
as You clear my mind.
The seas will flow
as You give me Your glow.

The old me will die,
the new me will fly.
Like an eagle I will soar,
with my wings I will adore
the One who opens every door.

Who will I be after You change me?
Who will I be after You rearrange me?

I will be fully Yours
as You reassure
my transformation will be complete.
Oh, how it will feel so sweet!

ABUNDANT BLESSINGS FROM A BROKEN SOUL

Therefore, if anyone is in Christ, the new creation has come: The old has gone, the new is here! – 2 Corinthians 5:17.

God makes us new. He transforms us from the old to the new. I wrote this as I was going through the program and envisioning what it would be like after my healing and transformation were complete. I was saved many years ago, but there I was talking about my depression. I lived with it for so long that it was my identity. I did not know who I was without it and that was scary for me. So I wrote this in the hopes that this will be the transformed me after God has healed me.

JOURNAL ENTRY

Write about your transformation, either when you were saved or a time God healed you from something and made you new.

_____

_____

_____

_____

_____

_____

_____

_____

ABUNDANT BLESSINGS FROM A BROKEN SOUL

PERFECTLY BROKEN

I'm perfectly broken,
my tears have spoken
of guilt, of shame
in which I felt the blame.

I tried to pick up my pieces
but never found the releases
from the pain that only increases.

Little by little, one by one,
each piece signifies something that can't be undone.

No matter how much I fight—
even with all my might—
I cannot do it alone,
I need to look to the throne.

As God picks up my pieces,
the pain finally decreases.
Little by little, one by one
for He has only begun.

His works are marvelous, wonderful, and true.
Can't I take that as my cue?

The pieces of my mind He has renewed.
The pieces of my body He has restored.
The pieces of my heart He has restarted.

I'm perfectly broken,
and it's not just a token.
That new refreshed angle
is just an example
of how He formed me—
fearfully and wonderfully made.

"Come to me, all you who are weary and burdened, and I will give you rest" — Matthew 11:28.

I wrote this poem one day after talking to a friend who said that I am "perfectly broken" and that really stuck with me. She was so right. I am right where God wants me so He can use me—every part of me. All the weird angles and shapes that make up me as a person all fit so perfectly together. You also, dear reader, are perfectly broken. All our pieces our Father picks up and then renews and restores.

JOURNAL ENTRY

Write about how you are perfectly broken and how you can use it to encourage and help others.

_____

_____

_____

_____

_____

_____

_____

_____

_____

EPILOGUE

We tend to look at our struggles and battles as the bad or negative things we have to endure in this life. We ask God, "Why me? Why do I have to go through this?" But in the end, God works it all out for His glory: "And we know that in all things God works for the good of those who love him, who have been called according to his purpose" (Romans 8:28).

During this writing process, I also had a revelation that our battles we walk through and receive breakthroughs from are not only for ourselves but also for our legacy. Our legacy can be our children, spiritual children, people we mentor, or lives we touch through our ministries. Our breakthroughs become our legacy's springboard, their platform so they can do greater things then we did. Just as Jesus said we would do greater things then He did: "Very truly I tell you, whoever believes in me will do the works I have been doing, and they will do even greater things than these, because I am going to the Father" (John 14:12).

Take your place in Christ not only in the good times, but also in the struggles and battles. Take your place! Walk through it all with all the grace God gives you. This last poem I wrote is called "Take Your Place," based on a revelation I had. I pray that it encourages you to step into all God has called you to do, not only for yourself, but for your legacy.

TAKE YOUR PLACE

"Take your place
In this space
and on this earth,
for what it's worth.

"Take your place
as you seek My face.
Through the battles
you will see what matters."

Stand in all God is calling you to do,
no matter the price,
don't think twice.
The Lord is at your side
and He will always provide.

The platform you give
for those after You to live,
the next generation,
will walk fully persuaded,
because of the breakthrough
you came through.

Your legacy you leave
will always achieve
far greater than you,
far greater—it's true.

So take your place
as God gives you grace.
So take your place,
at a steady pace.
And He will give you
much you can embrace.

Our victories surround us,
astound us,
and allow us
to encourage those
who come after us.

RESOURCES

NATIONAL ALLIANCE ON MENTAL ILLNESS
NAMI
WWW.NAMI.ORG

703-524-7600

FOCUS ON THE FAMILY
WWW.FOCUSONTHEFAMILY.COM

1-800-232-6459

NATIONAL SUICIDE PREVENTION LIFELINE
1-800-273-8255

*YOU CAN ALSO CONTACT YOUR LOCAL DOCTORS, THERAPISTS, COUNSELORS, AND CHURCHES FOR LOCAL RESOURCES.

PLEASE CONTACT LOCAL OR NATIONAL RESOURCES IF YOU ARE STRUGGLING AND NEED HELP.

Made in the USA
Middletown, DE
15 September 2022

10549252R00097